Hard Up

M.P. Carver

LILY POETRY REVIEW BOOKS

Contents

Love conquers all things except poverty and toothache.

—Mae West

At the Public Housing Complex, or, It Wasn't All Bad Until We Ran Out of Sky

That summer we made
our parents go check
the basement because
we swore we'd seen
a homeless guy sneaking
in and out. They didn't
find him or believe
us, but later a smelly bucket
proved we weren't lying.
I remember the landlord
would come rolling in
for a visit in a shiny car
each Sunday and park it
in our rusting sea
of jalopies. He didn't kick
anyone out for paying
late and got broken
appliances fixed right
away by his son-in-law
who came quick to hit
on all our single moms.
We were afraid to touch
the baby birds we found
chirruping in the backyard
bushes, and at night
bats came out to eat
mosquitoes, swooped right
down in front of our faces.
We learned to trick them
into going after any
small enough thing

thrown up into the air.
I wonder what those
poor bats thought
of it all? The toil, the
expectations, the pebbles?

If You Have Time To Lean

My first job
was at
McDonald's.

I took
counter orders
and worked

the drive thru.
They timed
everything

we did
and they had
cameras

always
on us
except

that time
the coffee pot
burst

on a Sunday
morning, and
Caitlyn ended

up in the ER
having shards
of glass

pulled out
with tweezers
and ointment

rubbed in
to soothe
her burns.

That day
the footage
disappeared

like a miracle
from the Lord
of corporate

boardrooms.
Tim McGraw
has a song

about
McDonald's.
A guy

who's lost
it all
(his all being

his house
his wife
his truck

his dog)
has to serve
the jerk

who took
it when
he comes

through the
drive-thru.
The lowest

point in this
guy's life
and there

I was
starting out
at fourteen

too young
to touch
anything but

the register.
McDonald's
said they

recorded us
for safety
but really

it was to
catch workers
stealing.

People still
stole
but I was

too scared.
In a typical
three-hour

lunch rush
I touched
over $2000

cash under
the blinking
Cyclopian eyes

of those cameras.
$21.75
of that

minus taxes
belonged
to me.

Why Do Teenage Girls Travel in Groups of 3, 5, or 7?

Because they literally can't even. My favorite joke.
I remember being a teenager, wandering around
with my friends at the Liberty Tree Mall, down
the street from our public housing complex.
All us mall rats were escaping something: empty
houses, screaming drunks, or just pain in the ass
families. At that age, the entire world seemed stupid,
unjust, and stacked against you. We never bought
anything except $2 pretzels at the Auntie Annes,
and the occasional Orange Julius. The authorities
hated us. They put up signs, No Unaccompanied
Minors in Groups of Five or More. How many peeps
in a posse? We laughed. We'd watch the mall cops
coming around to chase us away from-
the Suncoast, the Wet Seal, the Spencer's.
We broke apart and came back together,
a flock of starlings briefly startled by some
dumb, bumbling dog. Early 90s. Everything
seemed bright and clean then. Before ghost malls
and recessions. We were little gods of our
well-appointed domain. We didn't have money,
but we could bum around and be swept up
in our tidy, colorful, shoppable world just the same
as everyone else. Better, we knew every corner.
Knew, too, the old men, 20s and 30s, even 40s,
who hung around too long, trying to find the girl
whose home was worst, trying to look cool to an unwise
young rebel. This was before we got minimum
wage jobs like our parents, learned what it meant
to be broke and care. Before we understood
how that motel across the street behind the Denny's,
rented by the hour, stayed in business. Before overdoses.
Before whispering about which girl had fallen in
too deep to get out.

In the Parlor of the Blue-Collar Language Club

We open our pockets and find our mothers' tongues twisted up in the lint. We take them out to compare sharpnesses, admire their dank hums in the dim room. Back at home, we hang them again to dry like garlic. After all these years they are still wet. Drop by drop they drown the house. Later, we catch sight of one through the glare of a stranger's window. Our mouths swell with love.

My Friend's Mom Is CFO of Some Private Equity Holding Company; My Mom Sells Rings at the Mall

In her habitat she is apex, trapper,
catch and release a little lighter.
She glitters like a done-up but
affordable diamond shuffles the eye.
Let's try *dalliance*, let's try *dance*
—*retail* is an ugly word.

My mom makes the sale seem
like some half-remembered dream.
Not the dream about falling through the ice,
but the dream pulled out and fussed over,
'til it's so warm it shines.

CAPITALISM

My nephew's not even three yet,
but already he can spell some words
like S A L E and M A L L,
and I'm glad he's picking up
the finer nuances of capitalism
along with his letters.

If I can't give him a better world,
at least he can play with this one.
It's like when you buy toddlers
the best Christmas presents
and they spend the whole day
playing pretend with the box.

It's an ailing metaphor,
but modern culture's like the box.
I think of Ke$ha as a box.
I really like Ke$ha.
She's probably for sale
not that it does me any good.

If I could buy Ke$ha,
I don't think we'd be happy,
but we could both make-believe for a while.
We wouldn't even have to kiss,
but after we could sit side by side
and watch even the sun depreciate.

You Go Girl

If I lined up all my money in singles the long way
I'd have almost 1/10th of a mile of cash,

enough to take me from my door
to the candy aisle of the Walgreen's.

The short way, I can make it to the parking garage
but I can't pay the meter.

I have 988 grams of money,
or I would, if money weren't theoretical.

Instead I have pixels that the bank is loaning to me
in exchange for my money: Dear Green Hostage.

They are willing to negotiate, customer service says.
The ransom note must have been lost in the mail,

but I imagine they cut the letters from *Fortune* magazine
arranged them with an eye for aesthetics

then charged the cost of the materials, labor, a stamp
to my account — The Teller did it.

But I don't blame her. It was art. At last creativity,
a reprieve from the constant tally. She loved it.

It was a loss, but I've recalculated. I can still make it
to the sliding glass doors of the Walgreen's.

Employment

Carefully, I line up the six
bird spines, side by side
each vertebra balanced

on its left transverse
process, as close as I
can get them to a life-

like arch, just lying there
on the conference table.
Ever wonder where

the time goes?

The Rosetta Stone Girl

gave up on universal
language out of a hatred
for grammar drills: *I am.*

You are. She is
told to speak *motherese*
defined as simplified speech
with exaggerated intonation

and rhythm. But nothing
with her mother has ever been
simple. It shows when
nobody buys a box.

She thinks of companies
as those groupings of people
most united against her.
Mother Mother Mother

why must we spend
all our time tasting money?
What a complicated pronominal
structure, but it may reinforce

the buying decision.
If *you* cared as attentively
as you listen, you'd pick it up,
she gets commission.

The Corporate Assassin

Act 1. Scene 1. The Interview.

But what,
he asks,
do you do *here?*

We execute sales,
she says.

Listening to the Radio on the Ride Home from Work

It's chaos in there; a mangled retaining of defense attorneys, a collection of witness statements, dark accounting. An infinite loop of stories, of voices. When I turn away, they wink out like lights, or candles, or flames, or flash bulbs. The radio says that stars can also be ghosts, and we just can't tell the living from the dead. I don't believe this is true, I just think some stars are ignoring us. I forget each and every one of them, visible and unvisible, as I lay me down. In the morning, sun burning, I remember. Then forget. Then remember. Then forget

Market Strategies

In this story there is the grasshopper
and the ant.

The grasshopper doesn't work
but he's cooking a scheme to become his own bank
through strategic investment in whole life insurance
which he will fund by playing the middleman
hiring out that ant
who is naïve enough to toil away
for even minimum wage.

That ant—
as you may know—
spends night after night in therapy
discussing her compulsive swallowing of stars
growing luminous.

Welfare

Mencius said there is proof humans are good:
even a criminal, coming across a baby perched
near the edge of well, will snatch the baby back
without a thought. Then again, he was around
in 300 B.C. You could save a baby then, without
everyone asking *What the hell? Who are you*
to save that baby? There's paperwork associated
with that baby. Do you know how much that baby
is worth? Mencius's criminal lived in the Warring
States period, a good, well-defined time for folks.
Criminals were criminals, peasants were peasants,
the rich were rich, yes, even then, and anyone
could just walk around thoughtlessly saving babies.

Rich People Spend Their Money

on other money.
        I spend my money on string,

colorful string—
        looks good on the walls.

I have to be poor
        because

my mother was poor,
        so no one else

is helping to untie
        this legacy,

or even to hobble it—
        slice the hamstrings.

I wear it
        like a pretty toe ring

on my ugliest
        stubbiest toe,

the one that loves banging
        into bric-a-bracs

in rich-people houses.
        I like

to dent their things,
        so they'll appreciate them more,

instead of focusing
        on all that money.

Safe Travels

"Questions of reliability and robustness have to be answered before we leave Earth."
—Grant Anderson of Paragon Space Development Corporation

Billionaires have been reserving
tickets to Mars through SpaceX.
It could be possible within a decade
and I hope they get to go.

I won't make it to Mars,
but after a poetry reading
at the BPL the other day
I found myself in the IN crowd

at the afterparty at the Copley,
where a waiter brought me pillows
of pretzel skewered on plastic sticks
and I didn't even look at him,

though he could have been
my best friend, my student,
or my mom who used to cater
weddings at Spinelli's, at the head

table with the biggest tips.
When I worked in catering,
we'd convince people they needed
too much, then take most of it back

unopened at the end of the night.
On average, we sent out one can of coke
five times, a capitalist recycling.
On Mars, they are going

to have to recycle everything,
even the urine, and they won't
have soda, they'll drink
Soylent Interplanetary Formula.

When all the Billionaires go to Mars,
I'm really going to miss them.
And by the way I *love* Soylent.
You probably think I'm being sarcastic.

Apple News

Brazil is encouraging logging in the Amazon. Forest fires in California are killing even older, resilient redwoods. Cobalt and chocolate are made with slave and child labor, and hair extensions, and frozen oysters. Our iPhones are little bricks of guilt in our pockets, bright, app-y worlds we can carry. They chirp and sell us bedtime stories, show us how to buy. We had to make up and start using a term like post-truth. Fish have started breathing plastic, and the rich keep getting richer. So we screwed that up too.

We've Been Playing Monopoly Wrong

for Angela

Build houses and hotels
       with money from the bank.
Let friends and strangers
       stay for free.
Make the utilities public,
       pool properties. Photocopy
the Get Out of Jail Free card,
       share. Forgive rents
from Mediterranean to Boardwalk.
       Pass the dice
to all your friends and strangers.
       Top hats for all.
Take the Free Parking money,
       throw a party on Pacific,
put a sculpture park on Pennsylvania,
       a community center on Ventnor.
Get the railroads, and a whistle.
       Hop on, hop off.
we're all hobos now.
       Invite all your friends
and all your strangers.

       Pass Go.   Pass Go.   Pass Go.

Acknowledgments

Thanks to my friends and family, as well as the poets and mentors who have had a part in shaping these poems over the years. Too many to name, you know who you are.

Thanks also to the journals and anthologies who published the following poems from this manuscript:

"At the Public Housing Complex, or, It Wasn't All Bad Until We Ran Out of Sky", *9x5* (Anthology by Only Human Press)

"You Go Girl", *9x5*

"Market Strategies"; *Poetry South*

"C A P I T A L I S M", *9x5*

About the author

M.P. Carver is a poet and visual artist from Salem, MA. She is Director of the Massachusetts Poetry Festival, miCrO-Founder of *Molecule: a tiny lit mag,* and teaches creative and digital writing at Salem State University. Her work has been published in *Rattle, Mantis, Jubilat,* and *Love's Executive Order,* among others. She has received funding from the Massachusetts Cultural Council and the Essex Community Foundation. In 2023 her poem "In Vitro" was named a finalist in the Connecticut River Review's Experimental Poetry Contest, and in 2022 her poem "You & God & I" was awarded the New England Poetry Club's E.E. Cummings Prize. Her chapbook, *Selachipmorpha,* was published by Incessant Pipe in 2015.